AF483745

THERE'S MORE TO
HIPPOS
THAN YOU KNOW

25 Poems about Real Animals
with Hundreds of Fun Facts

David Parmelee

Illustrated by Maria DeCerce

an imprint of Sunbury Press, Inc.
Mechanicsburg, PA USA

an imprint of Sunbury Press, Inc.
Mechanicsburg, PA USA

Copyright © 2026 by David Parmelee.
Cover Copyright © 2026 by Sunbury Press, Inc.

Sunbury Press supports copyright. Copyright fuels creativity, encourages diverse voices, promotes free speech, and creates a vibrant culture. Thank you for buying an authorized edition of this book and for complying with copyright laws by not reproducing, scanning, or distributing any part of it in any form without permission. You are supporting writers and allowing Sunbury Press to continue to publish books for every reader. For information contact Sunbury Press, Inc., Subsidiary Rights Dept., PO Box 548, Boiling Springs, PA 17007 USA or legal@sunburypress.com.

For information about special discounts for bulk purchases, please contact Sunbury Press Orders Dept. at (855) 338-8359 or orders@sunburypress.com.

To request one of our authors for speaking engagements or book signings, please contact Sunbury Press Publicity Dept. at publicity@sunburypress.com.

FIRST SPECKLED EGG PRESS: April 2026

Set in Adobe Garamond | Interior design by Crystal Devine | Cover by Lawrence Knorr. Cover art and illustrations by Maria DeCerce | Edited by Debra Reynolds.

Publisher's Cataloging-in-Publication Data
Names: Parmelee, David, author.
Title: There's more to hippos than you know : 25 poems about real animals with hundreds of fun facts / David Parmelee.
Description: First trade paperback edition. | Mechanicsburg, PA : Speckled Egg Press, 2026.
Summary: Animals are fascinating, fun, and loveable. 25 charming (but still genuine) poems accompany hundreds of little-known fun facts about creatures of all kinds, as familiar as the bunny and as exotic as the hippo and the moray eel. Unique and quirky illustrations by a brilliant animal artist let children and adults see them as never before. Why not laugh while you learn?
Identifiers: ISBN 979-8-88819-370-9 (softcover).
Subjects: JUVENILE NONFICTION / Animals / General | JUVENILE NONFICTION / Poetry / Humorous | JUVENILE FICTION / Science & Nature / Zoology.

Designed in the USA
0 1 1 2 3 5 8 13 21 34 55

For the Love of Books!

*To our children, their children, and
all children whose hearts seek communion
with all our Creator has made.*

CONTENTS

ACKNOWLEDGMENTS

No thought, great or small, finds expression without friends and allies. To Sunbury Press, Lawrence Knorr, and crew, I am forever thankful. Many blessings.

PROLOGUE

And God said, Let the waters bring forth abundantly the moving creature that hath life, and fowl that may fly above the earth in the open firmament of heaven.

And God created great whales, and every living creature that moveth, which the waters brought forth abundantly, after their kind, and every winged fowl after his kind: and God saw that it was good.

And God blessed them, saying, Be fruitful, and multiply, and fill the waters in the seas, and let fowl multiply in the earth.

And the evening and the morning were the fifth day.

And God said, Let the earth bring forth the living creature after his kind, cattle, and creeping thing, and beast of the earth after his kind: and it was so.

And God made the beast of the earth after his kind, and cattle after their kind, and every thing that creepeth upon the earth after his kind: and God saw that it was good.

FURRY

THE BUNNY

The bunny bears no arms at all.
Its battle flag, a cotton ball.

All forms of self-defense it shuns
and, when advanced upon, it runs.

The bunny nation's gentle habits
demand they reproduce like rabbits.

Rabbits are called bucks and does, but their babies are kittens or kits.

They can turn their ears 180 degrees, and have almost 360-degree vision.

Their teeth never stop growing.

Rabbits can't vomit.

They can jump 3 feet high and run 18 miles per hour.

Bunnies can twist or kick in mid-jump. The trick is called a "binky."

A bunch of rabbits is called a herd.

Their noses are incredibly sensitive, with 100 million smell receptors.

The Eastern Cottontail rabbit was named because of its large white tail.

The oldest bunny lived to be 16.

Rabbits purr when they're happy, like cats.

Carrots aren't part of a wild rabbit's diet. A pet rabbit shouldn't eat a lot of them.

A rabbit's home is called a "warren." They dig rooms underground, connected by tunnels.

Some kinds of rabbits can weigh 20 pounds. The biggest ever weighed over 50 pounds!

Unlike most mammals, rabbits sleep with their eyes open. Sometimes they don't even lie down.

A mother rabbit can give birth to 12 or 14 kits at one time.

Scientists once thought rabbits were part of the rodent family, like squirrels and guinea pigs. They actually aren't.

They may seem very quiet, but rabbits can growl and grunt.

The loudest sound a rabbit can make is thumping its strong back legs against the ground.

BEAVER

Track this slow, determined fellow
when the leaves turn red and yellow.

Watch him chew for all he's worth
felling trees of massive girth
to build a home.

So should we all!

(What did <u>you</u> get done last fall?)

BEAVER

DID YOU KNOW?

Like mice, beavers are rodents—the largest in North America. In the entire world, only the capybara is larger.

Beavers are among the few animals that make big changes to their environment.

Beavers create ponds when they build dams across streams. The ponds help other local species survive.

The interior of a beaver lodge is about 4 feet across. The walls are a foot thick.

Their favorite foods include woody branches of birch and maple trees.

Beavers dig canals that allow them to float branches back to their lodges.

Beavers have 5 digits, like our fingers, on their front paws.

They can close their ears underwater. Their eyes feature nictitating membranes that close underwater but still allow them to see—a lot like goggles.

The world's heaviest beaver weighed over 100 pounds.

Every beaver's tail has a different size and shape.

Beavers steer with their tails. They also slap the water with them as a warning device, and store fat in them to help them survive over the winter.

They can swim at 6 miles per hour. Champion human swimmers reach 5.25 miles per hour.

Beaver moms carry their kits on their tails—and sometimes in their paws.

Beavers have an oil gland that helps keep their fur waterproof.

At one time there were 400 million beavers in North America alone!

Beaver teeth contain iron. That makes them look rusty—but way better for gnawing on trees.

Canada's national symbol is the beaver!

DACHSHUND

Dachshund's heart is filled with pride
though he's neither tall, nor wide.

He isn't blessed with gifts of strength,
of height, or girth, or width—

just length.

Respect the Dachshund, though; he's thorough
clearing out a badger's burrow.

Noble Dachshund, head held high,
trots briskly by,

and by,

and by.

The Dachshund was bred to hunt badgers, rabbits, and other creatures that live in burrows. That's why their legs are so short.

A Dachshund can be 5 to 9 inches tall.

Dachshund means "badger hound" in German.

The name is pronounced "DOKS hoont," not "DASH hound."

A dachshund will chase anything that's small, furry, or squeaks.

They are scent hounds. They rely on their noses to find things.

Their long, soft, floppy ears prevent dirt, grass, and other harmful things from getting inside their ears.

Dachshunds are in the top 10 most popular breeds in the US.

They are smart enough to learn a large number of commands and will obey them—whenever they feel like it!

Hot dogs used to be called "Dachshund sausages."

The first Olympic mascot was a Dachshund called Waldi, in 1972, when the Games were held in (you guessed it) Germany.

Dachshunds are one of the longest-living dogs. The oldest ones have lived over 20 years.

Dachshund races are held in many countries, even though they can't run very fast.

Most Dachshunds have very short hair, but there are long-haired and wire-haired versions, too. They look very different!

A walk in the rain or snow isn't much fun for a Dachshund. They're too close to the cold, wet ground!

For a smaller dog, they have a very deep, loud bark.

GIRAFFE

You chew the tender tops of trees
that no one else attempts
or sees.

A ratio of height to length
that scoffs at physics, tensile strength,

and all good taste.
A cut-and-paste.

Your neck should overweigh your feet!

(Your tail, at best, rates *Incomplete.*)

How do we calculate the force
It took for God to stretch a horse?

DID YOU KNOW?

Four species of giraffes have been found: Northern, Southern, Masai, and Reticulated.

Giraffes weigh a ton—literally.

The spots of each individual giraffe are like fingerprints. No two are the same.

The heart of a giraffe weighs 20 pounds. A human heart weighs about half a pound.

The giraffe is every bit as big as you think it is: 15–19 feet high. Their necks alone are as tall as a very tall human.

A giraffe baby's first moment is a six-foot fall to the ground.

One of the challenges of being so tall is getting a drink of water. A giraffe's neck is long enough to reach buds on the tops of trees, but too long to reach a pond or stream. The giraffe spreads its legs very, very wide to drink.

The leaves of the acacia tree are the favorite food of the giraffe. Their 18-inch long tongues help them avoid the spiky thorns to reach the tender leaves.

No animal sleeps as little as the giraffe. They only get an hour a day. They stay on guard to watch for predators.

Even though giraffes' necks are very long, they only have 7 vertebrae in their necks, like most mammals—and people. The vertebrae are nearly a foot long! Ours are 1–2 inches long.

Their blood vessels keep the blood from rushing to their heads when they bend down for a drink.

A giraffe's blood pressure is twice what a human's is. They need it to pump blood all the way up to their heads!

Giraffes are found only in Africa.

A herd of giraffes is called a "tower." It may have 20 members.

Giraffes sometimes talk to one another using sounds so low the human ear can't hear them. At night, they sing to one another that way.

A female giraffe, or "cow," will babysit the young ones in the tower while other females go out to find food.

A "bull," or big male giraffe, can weigh over two tons!

Wild giraffes live over 25 years. It's very hard to create the perfect home for them in a zoo.

Now and then, a giraffe will have twins. Usually, just one baby.

GIANT ANTEATER

Some animals eat meat; some, plants.
You—ants.

Bizarre? Perhaps, but that's just who
you are.

Congrats!

Of ants,
we have enough,
so if you stuff yourself,
Who'll mind?
It's fine. Eat up.
Deploy that Shop-Vac nose.

No challenge, I suppose,
when using claws
six inches long
to tear up anthills dusk till dawn. That's tough.
I wouldn't do it.

You're up to it.

If anyone can
eat ants

you can.

DID YOU KNOW?

Standing on its hind legs, a Giant Anteater is taller than the average human.

An anteater's sticky tongue can be 20 inches long.

Their eyesight is poor, but their sense of smell is outstanding.

They sleep more than half the time.

Anteaters can live for over 25 years.

Their amazingly large, bushy tail is used like a parasol to protect from the sun.

Though they have no teeth, giant anteaters consume up to 30,000 ants every day.

Using its 4-inch claws, an anteater can often defend itself from attack by a jaguar.

Anteaters don't secrete stomach acid. The ants they eat supply plenty of that.

A mother anteater usually has one baby and carries it on her back for a year.

The Latin scientific name for an anteater means "worm tongue."

The anteater's tongue isn't the longest of any animal. The blue whale's tongue holds the record at eight feet. But the anteater's is one of the longest—even longer than a giraffe's.

Anteaters also eat fruit. They tear it apart with their huge claws.

To find the next anthill, anteaters will swim quite a distance. They're good swimmers. They keep their long noses above the water like a snorkel.

If it needs to, an anteater can run 30 miles per hour for a short distance.

Of all the mammals, anteaters have the lowest body temperature: just under 90 degrees. Their insect diet doesn't provide a lot of energy.

Baby anteaters are called pups.

MEERKAT

Those who stand up in a bunch
risk becoming someone's lunch
when in the treacherous savannah.

And yet you stand, you
darling creature.
You'll be featured
on the cover!

Charming meerkat, you're the star
of all the arid Kalihari.
Strike that pose!
You're cute, Lord knows.

What's your posture, kat of meer,
When there's not a camera near?

DID YOU KNOW?

The meerkat is a type of mongoose—an animal known for its fearlessness.

Meerkats eat scorpions.

Meerkats are not much bigger than a squirrel.

Fossils have been found that are 2.5 million years old.

They are not endangered.

"Meerkat" is Dutch for "lake cat." Yet, they are a desert animal.

Their enemies include birds of prey, such as hawks and eagles.

A community of meerkats will set out sentries to watch for predators. They choose 3 levels of sentries based on age and experience.

Because they are so charming and photogenic, meerkats are often featured in movies.

Meerkats mob cobras, a highly venomous snake, to prevent them from striking individuals in the group.

Meerkats often play and wrestle with one another.

They weigh only 1–2 pounds, but can live up to 20 years.

A group of meerkats can be called a pack, a mob, or a gang. A pack includes about 30 animals.

Baby meerkats can be called cubs. It's a lot more fun to use their other name, "meerkittens!"

The meerkat diet includes just about anything: plants, insects, snakes, birds, small animals, and eggs. Since they live in the desert, occasional rain is important to them. As long as they have that, they do very well.

Snake venom has much less effect on meerkats than other animals. If they're bitten, they may get sick for a while, but they recover.

Meerkats are among the smartest animals—as smart as dogs or dolphins.

SLOTH

Just

go

slow
and you'll
be
fine.

So says the latest in a line
of sloths that stretches back for centuries

dodging problems,
penitentiaries,
tension, stress, and high anxiety

trading speed for calm sobriety,
clamped onto a bough.

But how
Can *I* shed care and worry?

Sloth: *No sweat.*

No hurry.

DID YOU KNOW?

The name "sloth" means "slowness." Something warm has warmth. Something long has length. Something slow has sloth (pronounced "slowth").

There are six kinds of sloths. They all live in Central America or South America.

Sloths are arboreal, meaning they live in trees.

A sloth can take a month to digest a meal of leaves.

A sloth can do a one-armed pull-up.

Sloths have either two or three toes. Their claws are 3–4" long to hold onto tree limbs.

10,000 years ago, giant sloths the size of elephants lived where modern sloths do now. They weighed as much as 7 tons.

Today's sloths live 20–40 years.

Baby sloths don't have a special name, like kittens or puppies. Some call them "slowbies."

Sloths spend most of their time hanging upside-down from tree limbs. When they do move, they are the world's slowest animals: .03 MPH.

Sloths sleep 8–10 hours a day, much like humans.

They swim three times faster than they move on land. They do the backstroke.

They come down to the ground to poop about once a week.

Algae often grows in their fur, giving them a greenish color that helps them hide in trees.

Sloths don't sweat, and have no natural smell. It's hard for predators to detect them.

Some kinds of sloths can turn their heads almost 360 degrees.

When sloths give birth, they move close to the ground so the baby will not be hurt if it falls. They rescue it if it does.

BORDER COLLIE

When do you find time to sleep?
You live for just one thing: *herd sheep.*
If any ewe has gone astray
. . . you're on your way!

What was that blur?
Your fur.

You'd think the sheep might solve the puzzle:
lots of them, and your lone muzzle
bossing them around.

You hug the ground
and do your creepy-creep.
Hey, sheep! Come at me, bro!

But no. Along they go.

You go get that wayward lamb.
Seems you're smarter than I am.

DID YOU KNOW?

"Collie" is the Scottish word for any kind of sheepdog.

Collies are highly intelligent.

They are workaholics. They aren't happy if they aren't working or herding.

They can be trained to herd geese as well as sheep.

One Border collie learned over 1,000 words.

They are the most agile, quick, and nimble dogs, and love to race obstacle courses.

Border Collies were bred from dogs brought to Britain by Romans or Vikings.

All Border Collies today are descendants of one dog who lived in the late 1800s.

The first herding competition or "trial" for Border Collies took place in 1873.

Queen Victoria of England and the great Scottish poet Robert Burns owned Border Collies.

Border Collies have an intense stare called the "Collie eye."

Border Collies hold the dog records for skateboarding, rolling down a car window, and walking while balancing a can on their heads.

They are very good at search and rescue. Trained Border Collies have found many lost people.

Movie directors love to work with Border Collies because they respond to commands so well. They often get film and TV roles.

Some Border Collies are definitely left-handed!

Even over rough, uneven ground, like a sheep or cow pasture, a Border Collie can hit 30 miles an hour.

Many Border Collie owners feel their dogs are smarter than they are! They can open doors and gates, find hidden snacks, always seem to figure out how to get what they want.

While they are often friendly to visitors, they truly love only one or two people.

ZEBRA

Is this a horse?
Of course!
But with a . . . pattern.

Dots and dashes?
Stripes.

Oh. Yipes.
I can't upload it.

No wonder no one's rode it!

DID YOU KNOW?

There are three kinds of zebras. All live in sub-Saharan Africa.

All zebras feature black-and-white stripes. Each animal has its own unique pattern, like a fingerprint.

They can run as fast as 40 MPH.

We don't really know why zebras have stripes. They may confuse predators, or help zebras recognize one another.

Zebras are constantly on the move seeking fresh grass and water. They can travel thousands of miles.

Zebras are a lot like horses, other than their coloring, but tend to be smaller and have much shorter manes.

Horses are not native to Africa, though they have been brought there.

One of the most common injuries to people on safari is a bite from a zebra.

Zebras have almost never been trained or domesticated like horses. They're much more aggressive, and more hostile to humans.

Like horses, they live in bands, with a stallion, several mares, and young foals.

Zebras can sleep while standing by locking their knee joints. They like to lie down to sleep when they feel safe enough.

When the foals are old enough, 1–3 years, stallions form their own bands.

Zebras defend against fierce predators such as lions, leopards, and hyenas by forming a circle, with their headquarters facing outwards. They kick with their hooves.

When a zebra is injured, others will surround and defend it.

OTTER

How much fun
for two young boys

is *mud?*
Who could have more?

Two otters can, along the shore
of murky streams—they'll roll about, kick, fight, and land
a punch.
Then break for lunch.

It's great.

I'd hate
to interrupt the slapping tails
and large incisors.

How good some mud and tussling was
before age made us wiser.

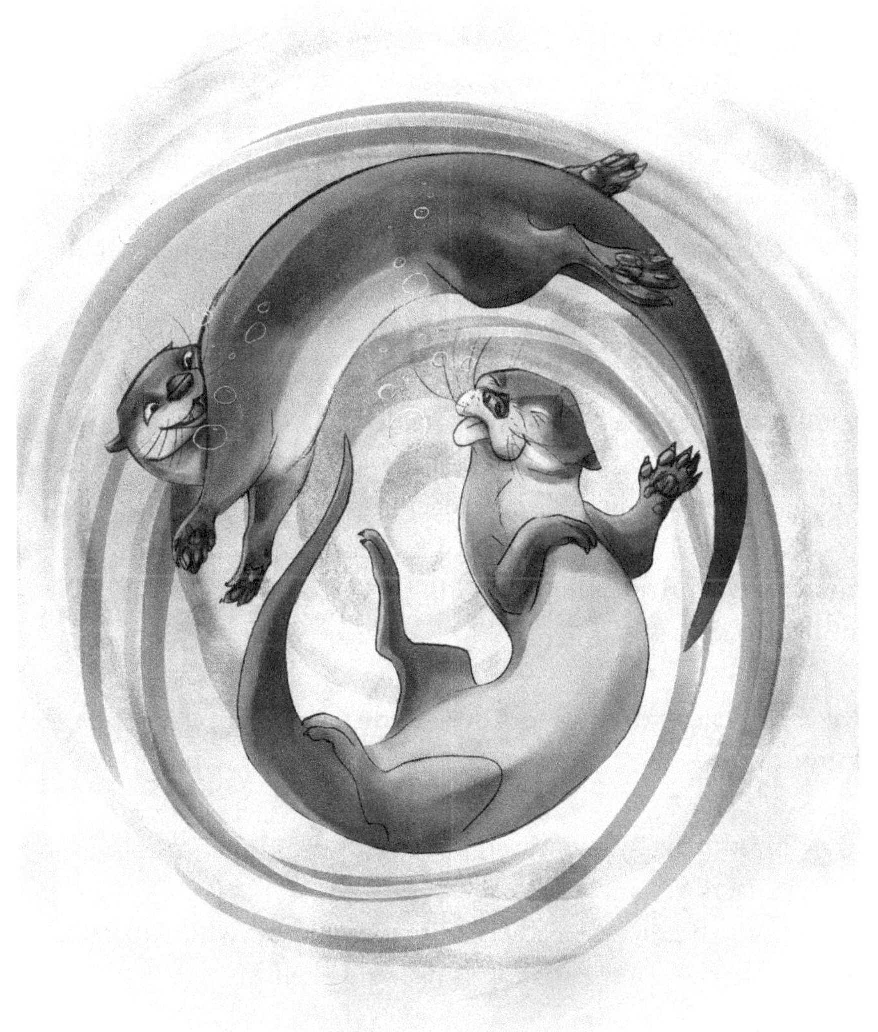

There are two kinds of otters: sea otters and river otters.

Sea otters weigh 50–100 lbs. They spend their lives in the sea.

River otters are much smaller, 20–25 pounds, and spend their time partly on land.

River otters are social. The play and wrestle together, and communicate with chirps and whistles.

Otters often hold hands while sleeping.

You can tell a river otter by its long, sleek body, powerful tail, and webbed feet.

River otters can dive 60 feet deep and stay underwater for 8 minutes.

They build dens by the water, lined with moss and grass.

Otters put their food on their stomachs and eat while floating on their backs. They eat a lot of fish and shellfish.

River otters can run 15 miles per hour, and use slippery surfaces such as mud or ice to go even faster from place to place. The average human can run about 6 miles per hour.

River otters travel 10–20 miles a day to find their favorite foods.

They have 36 teeth and strong jaws for eating food such as shellfish and mollusks.

They have the densest fur of any mammal: one million hairs per square inch. The average house cat has about 60,000.

The only continents without otters are Australia and Antarctica.

Otters are part of the weasel family. They're not only the biggest, but the only ones that live mainly in the water.

A group of otters on land is called a "romp." At sea, it's called a "raft."

The Giant River Otter found in the Amazon River is 6 feet long!

Otters often take over dens made by other animals, like beavers and muskrats. Sometimes they move in while other animals are still there.

FURRY & FIERCE

COYOTE

Slink down. *Crouch low.*
Stealthily arrive, then go.
Unexpected—undetected.
Snatch that chicken, unprotected.

Pups are howling: feed us, Daddy!
Bring the good stuff with the bad—he said
that he'd be back by morning.

Farmer's rifle fires a warning.

Deftly dodge the angry bullet
Manage one more time

to pull it off,
coyote, lean grey ghost.

Are you honest?

Well—*almost.*

DID YOU KNOW?

Coyotes are members of the dog family but not domesticated like dogs.

They prefer to live in the open desert or prairie but can be found very close to people's homes.

Coyotes live in family groups called packs of 5 or 6, plus new pups. They're often seen traveling or hunting, alone or in pairs.

Coyotes are smaller than grey wolves and red wolves.

They are highly intelligent, and very good hunters.

They sleep out in the open unless they have pups. If they do, they borrow a burrow made by another animal such as a raccoon.

Many people believe coyotes raid garbage cans or prey on pets. They really don't. Coyotes mainly eat small wild animals, as well as larger ones such as deer.

Native Americans often told stories in which a coyote became a clever trickster who could fool other animals, or even humans.

The most famous coyote is Wile E. Coyote, a character in Looney Tunes cartoons who's been chasing a roadrunner unsuccessfully since 1949. He almost never speaks.

Though they aren't dogs, coyotes are often called "song dogs" because of the loud, high-pitched howling of the pack. It can reach 120 decibels and be heard for 3 miles in open terrain.

North and Central America are home to 19 different kinds of coyotes.

People once thought coyotes howled at the moon. They really don't. They howl when the moon is out because that's the best time for them to hunt. The pack communicates by howling while hunting together.

Barking, yipping, growling, and laughing are other sounds coyotes use to speak to one another. Their laugh often keeps campers in coyote territory awake at night!

Coyotes can even scream like a human. People who have never heard their scream often think someone is in trouble nearby.

It's not a good idea to put out food for coyotes near your home. They are shy, and avoid people whenever they can. The food convinces them to come closer than they should.

A mother coyote gives birth to 3–12 pups.

Even a city can be a pretty good home for a coyote if it loses its natural habitat. When that happens, they are forced to scavenge for food, often in garbage cans, and develop a bad reputation.

HYENA

Not a dog, not a wolf
You find some way to feed yourself
in every season, fat or lean

You're mean.

In pick-up packs, you track the smell:
springbok, eland or gazelle
(it's meat)

through heat
of day, or gloom of night.

No fight.
Just wait. Then pounce,
and not an ounce remains
when you are done.

The sun
reveals the scene:
hyenas gone. Picked clean.

Your adjective?
Relentless.

The free buffet is endless.

DID YOU KNOW?

Hyenas aren't "wild dogs." They're a different animal altogether.

Hyenas are famous for being scavengers, but they can hunt on their own, too.

They are pack animals, who communicate exceptionally well.

They're not afraid of many other animals, but they do fear lions.

The movie *The Lion King* made them look really bad.

They're smarter and solve problems better than most animals—even chimpanzees.

Hyenas have one of the strongest bites in the animal kingdom. They can crush bones to eat the marrow inside.

The howl of the hyena is mentioned in the Book of Isaiah in the Old Testament.

Females are larger and more aggressive than males.

Hyenas aren't part of the dog or cat family. They're closer to cats, and developed from cats millions of years ago.

Hyenas can growl, whoop, cackle, and giggle. The "laughing hyena" really does laugh, but not when they're happy—only when they're threatened or frustrated.

Hyenas can chase their prey at 40 miles an hour for one or two miles.

Because their stomachs can hold 30 pounds of meat, hyenas can go for days without eating.

A clan of hyenas is made up of 5 to 80 animals.

A large female hyena can weigh 180 pounds, as much as all but the largest dogs.

Hyena mothers spend more time and energy with their cubs than any other land mammal does.

Hyenas are some of the most intelligent animals. They are as clever as chimpanzees in solving problems, and very curious!

SCALY

CHAMELEON

Pick a hue!
We just can't find you.

Indecisive. That defines you.

Jack of all the tonal trades
Master of so many shades,
stays protected by confusion
choosing to employ illusion,
being short on teeth and claws.

I just saw him—let us pause
and search the plant life for his presence:

He's there. I swear.

Wait—*now he isn't!*

DID YOU KNOW?

Their name comes from two ancient Greek words that mean "ground lion," because of a crest some have on their heads.

A quarter of all chameleon species live on Madagascar.

They can live only in very warm climates.

They live in deserts, rainforests, and mountainous regions.

Chameleons can see in a full circle around themselves.

They don't actually change color to match their surroundings. Their color depends on their mood, the temperature, and humidity.

They can spot prey almost 30 yards away.

Chameleons can be as small as one inch, or as large as 28 inches.

They live 2–10 years.

Their sticky tongues reach out to catch prey—mainly bugs. They are twice as long as the chameleon's body.

Chameleon tails are prehensile, meaning they are used like arms and legs. They can twist their tails around a branch to help them hang on to a tree.

Chameleons live mainly in trees.

Baby chameleons survive on their own from the time they're born.

Chameleons can see ultraviolet light.

Their five toes help them hang on to branches when they catch prey with their powerful tongues.

Chameleons appeared on earth just after dinosaurs became extinct.

They are solitary creatures.

KOMODO DRAGON

Fearsome creature.
Such a reputation!

You only have them
in your nation
if you live
on certain islands,
like Komodo,
Rinca, Flores.

Lock your doors
If you do. Dragons
don't like you.

They lack the fiery breath
that *real* dragons boast
(they can't make toast.)

Instead, they prowl the jungles on stout legs
to lay their eggs
two dozen at a time, in batches.

Each Dragon knows the deal when it hatches.
Climb a tree.
Get way up in the air.

It's dangerous down there.

DID YOU KNOW?

The Komodo Dragon is the world's largest living lizard, up to 10 feet long and 300 pounds.

They live only on certain islands in Indonesia.

Scientists didn't know about them until 1912.

Komodo Dragons eat deer, wild pigs, goats, and other Komodo dragons.

Deer make up most of their diet.

A dragon's powerful tail is as long as its body. It can knock down a deer.

They grow five sets of 60 teeth in their lifetimes.

They are venomous. The glands are between their teeth.

Young dragons live in trees to avoid being eaten.

Local people call them "land crocodiles."

They swim for miles along the shore to reach another nearby island.

They have bony armor in their skin.

Komodo Dragons lay eggs, which they incubate for eight months.

They are very popular in zoos.

Dragons can live to be 35.

They are very fast—13 miles an hour when hunting.

As fierce as they are, Komodo Dragons are endangered because of their very small habitat. Only about 1500 remain.

Though they will often eat together, Komodo Dragons are solitary most of the time.

Komodo Dragon fossils have been found in Australia. They don't live there anymore.

A Komodo Dragon inspired the 1933 movie King Kong.

CROCODILE

A ghastly set of teeth
attached
to scaly bits.
Bad fits.

He sure could use
some decent orthodontia.
Still, he'll chomp ya
With no provocation,
stationed
on the muddy bottom of the Congo,
the Zambezi, or the Nile.

He whiles away his hours
awaiting prey.
At times, all day.

Croc-o-dile, we do

(pray we don't meet you.)

Crocodiles have lived on earth for over 200 million years.

They are a living link to dinosaurs.

A saltwater crocodile can weigh over a ton and measure 40 feet long.

They live in swamps, lakes, and rivers.

Crocs have excellent vision and hearing, and an even better sense of smell.

They mainly eat fish, but will eat almost anything: turtles, snakes, buffalo, wild boar, and crabs.

They can live to be 70 or more.

Crocodiles communicate with grunts, hisses, roars, and whistles.

Crocodiles lay eggs. When the young hatch, they are about a foot long.

Crocodile hide is in great demand for handbags and shoes.

They spend a lot time regulating their temperature because they are cold-blooded. This includes basking on riverbanks in the shade, and sitting motionless with their mouths wide open.

The eyes, ears, and nostrils of a crocodile can be above the water when the rest of its body is submerged.

They use their powerful tails to swim.

Crocodiles rarely attack humans.

The only continents with no crocodiles are Europe and Antarctica.

The only crocodile predators are jaguars, leopards, anacondas, pythons, and other crocodiles.

Meat makes up most of a crocodile's diet, but they also love fruit, and eat a lot of it!

Crocs hunt mainly at night. They sneak up on their prey silently and attack with lightning speed.

Each of a crocodile's 80 or so teeth can be replaced 50 times over its lifetime.

WATERY

PIRANHA

Nasty fish.

He'll bite ya—*don't fall in!*
He, and his kin,
bring major troubles.

(See the bubbles?)

Watch the surface churn.
The school shows what they learn
as guppies: chew 'em up.
It's gone in sixty seconds. Fast and furious.

Soon, you're curious:
Where's my cow?

And how
can they all dine so fast?
A minute passed,
and all that's left is bones!

Who owns
a set of teeth like those?

Piranha knows.

Piranhas are found in South American freshwater rivers.

They live in large groups for safety.

They communicate by grinding their teeth, and by making a barking or drumming sound using their swim bladders.

Piranhas can detect even a tiny amount of blood in the water.

Piranhas eat almost anything, but mainly fish and shellfish.

They are only 5–12" long.

Piranhas have one row of extremely sharp teeth. They shed and regrow them their entire lives.

They have the strongest bite of any small fish. They can eat any sort of fish they find.

President Teddy Roosevelt visited Brazil in 1914 and saw extremely hungry piranhas in action. He called them "ferocious."

Despite the scary reputation of the piranha, they rarely bite humans. Almost no one has died from a piranha attack.

The legend about piranhas eating large animals in minutes really isn't true, though they will attack many kinds of animals.

People do catch and eat piranhas.

A group of piranhas is called a "shoal" because of the way they swim together perfectly as a group.

Though they are fierce when they're eating, piranhas are naturally shy and easily startled, even in a group.

A piranha's teeth are as hard as a shark's teeth.

There are at least 30 different kinds of piranhas of many different colors.

Different species of piranhas are being discovered all the time.

They live to be 10 years old—some as long as 25!

South American tribes who live near piranhas use their sharp teeth to make tools.

EEL

Eel, you feel
so like your name.
Forgive us, but it's true;

Creepy, crafty, slippery, sneaky.

Winding in and out
of leaky ports
in oceans blue.
That's *you.*

Does it surprise you,
watery genie,

that you would be
first-rate sushi?

ANOTHER EEL

I'm no fish. You get that, right?
And also—not a snake,

who lives in burrows, under rocks, in fields,
but not lakes
and rivers. Snakes give you the shivers,
don't they?
So I might,
If you could see me. But I'm sneaky, lurking
out of sight
behind a boulder, near the banks.
Give thanks.

Anacondas
live in rivers, you point out.
They ply the Amazon
In great reptilian arcs,
Nose above the water.
As they oughta.

They must have air, you see.

Not me.

DID YOU KNOW?

Although they look a lot like snakes, eels are fish.

Many types of eels live in fresh water but return to salt water to spawn.

Eels can breathe through their skin as long as they keep wet. This allows them to travel as much as 2000 miles through shallow water to rivers and oceans.

Eels can swim backwards. Try that yourself!

Eels can be as small as 4 inches and as large as 12 feet.

The oldest eels in captivity are 85 years old.

There are 200 species of Moray eels.

The bite of a Moray is not only nasty, but often toxic. Half the species produce mild venom that's harmful to humans.

Morays have a second set of jaws in their throats, with teeth. When they bite onto a fish, the second jaws rotate forward and pull it into their throats.

They don't see very well. They rely on smell instead.

Morays are excellent hunters. They often team up with other fish such as grouper to pursue their prey.

HIPPOPOTAMUS

Half boulder, half jaws
(plus rows of most imposing molars)

Sink to the riverbed, then pause
to wait for those who do not know you're
there.

A snare.

You lack the pointy bits
that raise alarm.
No harm
can come from such a roly-poly guy.

Oh, no? Hey, bro—
There's more to hippos than you know.

DID YOU KNOW?

"Hippopotamus" means "river horse" in Greek.

The hippopotamus is probably the third-largest living land mammal, after the elephant and rhino.

They weigh 3.5 tons and are 12'–18' long. It may be the second-largest. The rhino is similar in size and weight. We don't know for sure.

Despite their size, hippos can run almost 20 mph for 200 meters—the same as a champion 200-meter human runner.

They produce an oily pink substance that acts as sunblock, filtering UV.

Theirs hide are 2" thick at the thickest point.

Hippos love to bask in rivers, half-submerged, to stay cool and rest from carrying all that weight around.

They don't sweat.

Hippos dehydrate quickly out of water.

Their lower canine teeth are 12"–18" long.

Hippo poop helps the growth of fish, which people catch and eat.

Hippos eat 80 pounds of grass every night. They don't need as much food as other large animals because they float in the river during the day, conserving energy.

Hippo calves weigh 50–100 pounds.

Calves can cover their nostrils and ears to nurse underwater.

Hippos can live 40 years in the wild.

Almost all hippos live in Africa, but you can find 80 of them in Colombia. A few escaped from a zoo and formed a herd.

There are "Pygmy Hippos," but they aren't small: 6 feet long and 500 pounds!

Hippo teeth are made of ivory, like an elephant's tusks, but even harder.

Even though they live in water most of the time, hippos can't swim! They sink, then gallop along the bottom.

Young hippos practice their fighting skills on each other. (Not so different from grade school!)

OCTOPUS

So entirely unlike us,
the oddly-structured octopus:

—Eight legs.
—Can't sink.
—Creepy suckers.
—Cloudy ink.

Lurks in watery caves and niches
Dines on unsuspecting fishes

Curly tentacles for gripping
plus a beak (for basic ripping).

Dining out, Italians eat you.

May I, rather, *just not meet you?*

A SECOND OCTOPUS

with Maeve

Octopus's legs are great
in number: six. Or five? *Or eight?*
Or seven?

While it's large, and round
The octopus won't make a sound.

DID YOU KNOW?

There are 300 different kinds of octopuses.

Octopuses have three hearts. Two are used only for circulating blood to its gills.

Their blood is blue because of its copper content.

Swimming is extremely tiring for an octopus. They prefer to crawl.

Octopuses like to attack their prey by lurking in underwater crevices.

An octopus squirts ink to escape from predators. It forms a smokescreen while burning the attacker's eyes and disabling its sense of smell.

All octopuses are venomous, but only one type is dangerous to humans.

"Octopuses" is the best way to talk about more than one. People once thought "octopus" was a Latin word (though it isn't). In Latin, the plural would be "octopi," like "Gladiolus" and "Gladioli." Either word is OK.

Octopuses are silent. They don't make a sound.

The octopus can be curious about humans and interact with them safely. It's best not to come in contact with them, because their tentacles can harm human skin.

SHARK

That fin—!
A dolphin?
No.

A tall fin, cruising low,
below the chop.

A shark! Hop
out, right quick
and park yourself
up on the sand.

You'll see things differently
from land.

DID YOU KNOW?

Like rays, skates, and octopuses, sharks have cartilage instead of bone.

Sharks don't make a sound.

Sharks have fantastic vision, even at night. They can see colors.

They cruise at about 5 miles per hour, the speed of the fastest human swimmers. When they attack, most can swim more than 12 mph. Mako sharks are much faster.

There are 1,000 different kinds of sharks.

The hammerhead shark uses its head to pin stingrays to the sea floor before eating them.

Sharks can sense electrical signals in the water, helping them hunt.

Almost all sharks must keep moving to circulate water to their gills.

Sharks lose and replace their teeth constantly—as many as 35,000 in their lifetimes.

Humans kill 100 million sharks a year, mainly by fishing. Sharks kill about 5 people.

Sharks live in every ocean, and some lakes and rivers.
Some sharks lay eggs. Others give birth to live young.

Shark skin feels like sandpaper.

Some sharks glow in the dark.

A great white shark eats 10 tons of food a year. Humans eat
1–2 tons.

Sharks migrate thousands of miles over a long period of time.

Sharks can eat whales—and other sharks.

BUGGY

CENTIPEDE and MILLIPEDE

Centipede, raise your right hands—
and Millipede—you, too.

Please the court, tell us the truth
so we'll remember who is whoth.

You're both so slithery, creepy, icky
if we're forced to pick, we
might confuse you two.
We do.

Even on the bottom a shoe.

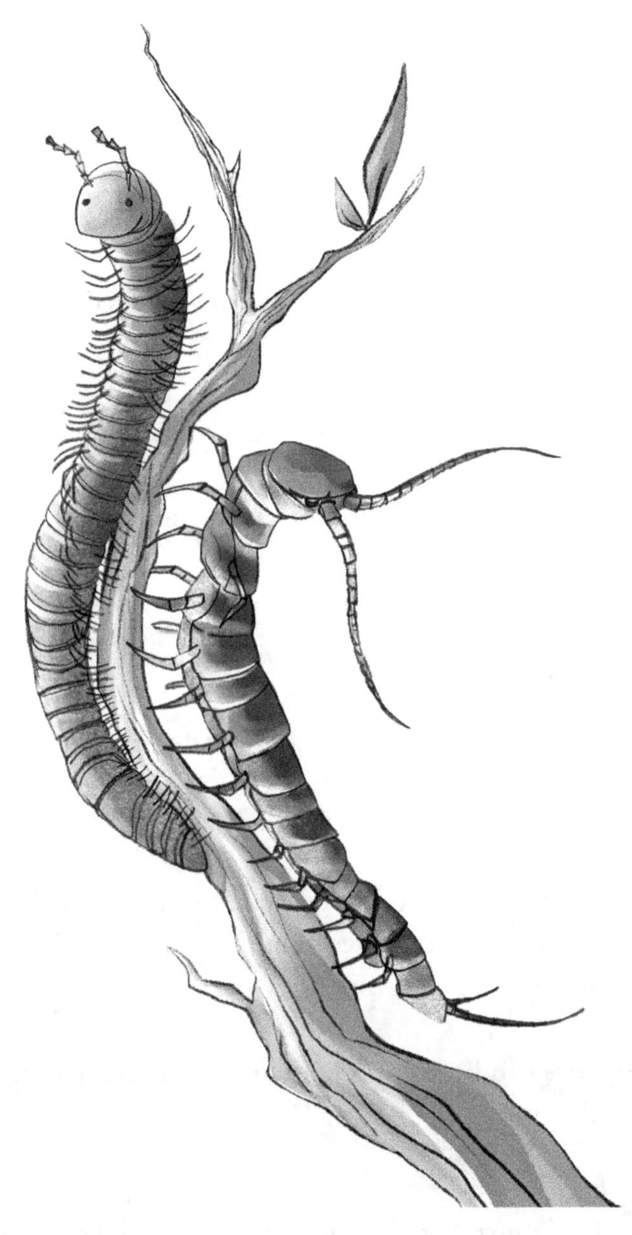

DID YOU KNOW?

There are 8,000 species of centipedes all over the world.

They can live to be five years old!

Centipedes eat worms and bugs if they're small, and birds or amphibians if they're larger.

Some centipedes live near the Arctic Circle.

They are venomous. However, their venom has almost no effect on humans.

"Centipede" is Latin for "hundred legs," but the number of legs a centipede actually has varies from 14 to 176. They have a pair of legs for every body segment.

They can be 10 inches in length.

Centipedes grow more legs every time they molt. If attacked by a predator, they can shed their legs to escape. Then they add more legs the next time they molt.

Centipedes can become dehydrated. That's why they live in damp places.

Millipedes aren't insects. They are closer to lobsters and crayfish.

Millipedes don't bite or sting.

 The U.S. has over 1000 species in every single state, including Alaska.

"Millipede" is Latin for "thousand legs." Most millipedes have nowhere near that many. It just looks that way. 400 is the usually the maximum number. Most have 100 or fewer.

Millipedes were some of the first creatures to live on land.

They are round in shape.

There are over 7,000 species worldwide.

One species of millipede glows in the dark.

They love rotting leaves and wood and help to turn them into compost.

Millipedes can be up to a foot long.

They can live as long as 10 years.

They have "stink glands" that protect them from predators. Wash your hands right away after handling one.

MOSQUITO

Mission:

Infiltrate my tent tonight, high-frequency invader
Find a meal, lay some eggs, retreat, then…come back later.

Master of the nighttime raid, her lighting undetected
Searching out uncovered spots, an elbow unprotected.

Salivate, then plunge in straight, the perfect spot selected
Leave a lump, a rising bump, with skeeter spit injected

If somehow I kill you with a satisfying thud,
what do you leave on my arm?

My own blood!

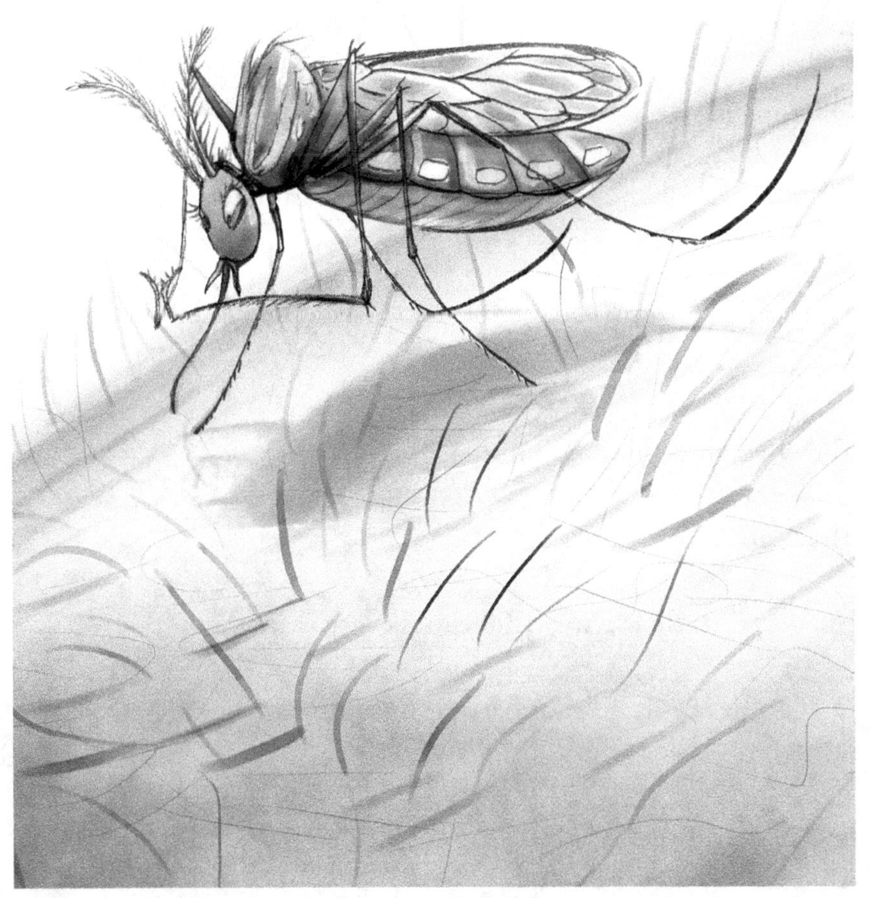

DID YOU KNOW?

Mosquitoes live almost everywhere in the world.

There are 3,700 different kinds.

Mosquitoes have been found at elevations above 8,000 feet in the Himalayas.

Only female mosquitoes bite.

Mosquitoes use their antennae to detect carbon dioxide given off by humans.

Mosquitoes use heat sensors to detect the warmth of the blood inside your body.

They live only about a month.

They can walk on water.

Females beat their wings 500 times every second.

Dragonflies eat large numbers of mosquitoes. They're sometimes called "mosquito hawks."

Females lay as many as 300 eggs at a time, in standing water. An inch of water is enough.

Mosquitoes can fly 1–2 mph.

Crane flies look like very large mosquitoes, but they don't bite.

The chemical DEET is the best mosquito repellent. They don't like the smell of it.

10% DEET can protect you against mosquitoes for about 90 minutes.

Male mosquitoes would rather eat nectar from flowers than bite people.

Mosquito eggs can live in a dry location for 8 months in cold weather and still hatch in the spring.

Two kinds of mosquitoes don't bite humans at all. One prefers birds. The other bites only dogs.

Almost every other kind of insect flies faster than mosquitoes, including bees and butterflies.

Some people don't react to mosquito bites at all. Others never get bitten. We don't understand why.

BUMBLEBEE

See the droning bumblebee,
a humble creature.
Hovering, his finest feature.

Cannot fly, say some professors,
(most in Physics).

Not a problem, is it?
No.
Just go.
He does.

Buzz buzz.

Bumblebee won't say, "I told you so," although
he's earned the right.

Instead, just look here: *flight.*

BUMBLEBEE

DID YOU KNOW?

There are over 250 species of bumblebees.

Bumblebees live on pollen. They can grab a flower with their jaws to shake the pollen loose.

Because bumblebees carry pollen wherever they go, they pollinate plants and crops to help them grow.

A bumblebee colony has 50 to 500 members.

Bumblebees don't store honey like other bees.

At the end of the season, the lives of the queen and the worker bees end. New queens hibernate through the winter and start new colonies when warm weather returns.

Bumblebees can fly in cooler temperatures than other kinds of bees. They shiver to keep warm, just like humans.

A bumblebee has five eyes.

Bumblebees can make their nests in a tree, a stone wall, a hole in the ground, or an abandoned rodent's nest.

They know which flowers have the most nutritious pollen.

Badgers, skunks, bears, raccoons, and some birds eat bumblebees.

Some have red stripes.

Their wings beat 200 times a second.

Male bumblebees don't sting.

Bumblebees live only about a month.

Dry, dark places underground are the favorite nesting spots for bumblebees. The queen looks for the best spots in springtime.

If you like seeing bumblebees in your yard or garden, you can attract them by planting crocuses, sunflowers, daisies, basil, and parsley.

Bumblebees flap their wings back and forth, instead of up and down like most insects and birds. They're a lot like helicopters.

ABOUT THE AUTHOR

DAVID PARMELEE is a Brown '79-educated author, playwright, director, actor, and former op-ed columnist (*The Times-Leader*, Wilkes-Barre, Pennsylvania) whose work includes a Civil War-era historical novel (*The Sea Is a Thief*, Sunbury Press), two upper-grade children's books (*Miss Feesenschneezen Is Ill* and *Miss Feesenschneezen is Fit*, both with illustrator Maria DeCerce, Sunbury Press), and a travel guide (*The Traveler's Guide to Chincoteague and Assateague*, Sunbury Press). He is also the author of 13 one-act plays, all produced by Little Theatre of Wilkes-Barre, Pennsylvania, Gaslight Theatre, and the Scranton Fringe Festival, Scranton, Pennsylvania. He and his wife Toni Jo live in northeast Pennsylvania. Their four adult children are making their way in the world.

ABOUT THE ILLUSTRATOR

MARIA DECERCE is an illustrator, designer, and animal lover. She has been illustrating children's books for more than a decade. *There's More to Hippos Than You Know* is her third collaboration with author David Parmelee. In addition to illustrating books, she is a graphic designer through her studio M.DeCreative LLC, and is the founder of an equestrian lifestyle brand, Weird Horse Girl Co. She lives in the middle of the desert in Arizona with a dog, a pony, three cats, an undisclosed number of chickens, and her partner Steven.

www.ingramcontent.com/pod-product-compliance
Lightning Source LLC
Chambersburg PA
CBHW071334130726
47996CB00002B/750